Bla

with

Music Theory!

by **Maureen Cox** Edited by **Victoria McArthur**

[Book 2]

Production: Frank and Gail Hackinson
Consulting Editors: Carol Matz, Edwin McLean, and Lucy Warren
Design and Art Direction: Terpstra Design, San Francisco
Illustration: Brian Conery
Engraving: Tempo Music Press, Inc.
Printer: Tempo Music Press, Inc.

THE
F·J·H
MUSIC
COMPANY
INC.
Frank J. Hackinson

First published 1988
by Subject Publications
    7 Bishops Court
    Wallace Road
    Broadstone
    Dorset BH18 8NF Great Britain
    Tel: 44 1202 567266
    Fax: 44 1202 467895
Revised 1990
New edition 1994
Fourth impression 1998

ISBN-13: 978-1-56939-085-6

For Michael

Note to Students

If you want to play your instrument correctly, sing well, or just improve your musical enjoyment, you will want to read music and understand its theory.

This book guides you through the theory of music in a simple, straightforward way. There are many pictures and interesting activities along the way. You will find a variety of challenging puzzles and questions to test your understanding. At the end of the book there is a dictionary of musical terms, a list of signs, and a progress chart for you to fill out.

As you learn more about music, I hope that you will discover that theory is fun.

Maureen Cox

Acknowledgments

I am extremely grateful to
Dr. Victoria McArthur for so skillfully
editing and revising this version of
Blast Off with Music Theory! I should
also like to thank Frank Hackinson, the
president of The FJH Music Company
Inc., for undertaking the publication
and distribution of these books
throughout the United States, Canada,
and South America. Finally, I should
like to express my gratitude to Fiona
Elliott and Lum Fun Lee for their
helpful comments, and to Dr. Marjorie
Brown-Azarowicz for her
encouragement and advice.

Maureen Cox

Contents

FJH1170

Major Key Signatures

In Book 1, you learned 3 key signatures:
C, **G**, and **F**

C major has no sharps or flats.
G major has an F♯.
F major has a B♭.

Fill in the letter name
for each key signature.

___ **major**

___ **major**

___ **major**

New Major Key Signatures

Here are the new major key signatures for Book 2.

D major has 2 sharps: F♯ and C♯.

A major has 3 sharps: F♯, C♯, and G♯.

B♭ major has 2 flats: B♭ and E♭.

E♭ major has 3 flats: B♭, E♭, and A♭.

Notice that the sharps and flats are always written on exactly the same lines and in the same spaces for all key signatures.

FJH1170

Major Key Signatures in Treble Clef

Write these key signatures in the **treble clef**. (Look back at pages 6 and 7 if you need help.) Remember to draw the clef sign!

G major

D major

A major

F major

B♭ major

E♭ major

Major Key Signatures in Bass Clef

Write these key signatures in the **bass clef**. (Look back at pages 6 and 7 if you need help.) Remember to draw the clef sign!

G major

D major

A major

F major

B♭ major

E♭ major

When you think you know these key signatures, turn the page and test yourself.

FJH1170

Writing Major Key Signatures In Both Clefs

Now you should be able to write key signatures with up to 3 sharps and 3 flats. Can you write them correctly in the treble and bass clefs below?

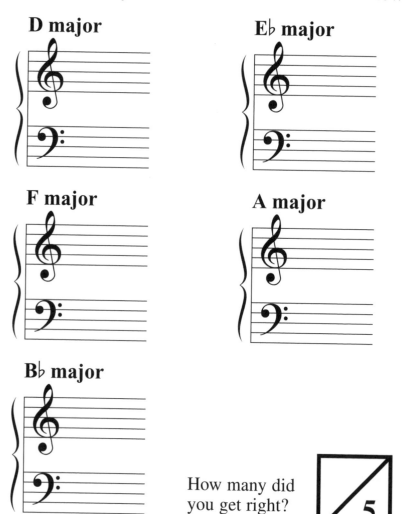

D major

E♭ major

F major

A major

B♭ major

How many did you get right?

⬜ /5

Half and Whole Step Review

In Book 1, you learned about half and whole steps by using a keyboard.

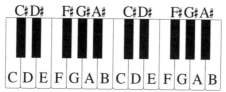

Use the keyboard drawing above to help you fill in the answers below.

Remember: A whole step is made up of 2 half steps.

1. F raised a half step is _____.

2. F♯ raised a whole step is _____.

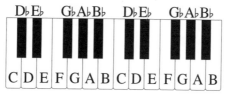

Use the keyboard drawing above to help you fill in the answers below.

3. A♭ lowered a half step is _____.

4. F lowered a whole step is _____.

Before turning the page, study the keyboard drawings above. On the next page you will try to fill in the letter names for all the keys.

FJH1170

Sharps and Flats
on the Keyboard

Write the letter names of all the black
keys *above* the keyboards.

On this keyboard, use **sharp names** for
the black keys.

C♯

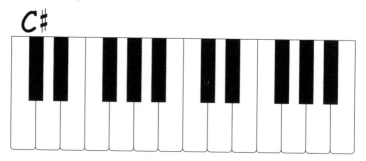

On this keyboard, use **flat names** for
the black keys.

D♭

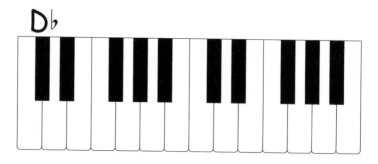

Half Steps in Major Scales

In every major scale, there is a half step between notes 3 and 4, and notes 7 and 8.

Here is a new scale for you: **A major**.
The half steps are marked with ∧ .

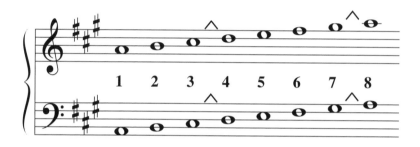

Write the key signature for A major. Then write the scale of A major **ascending** (going up).
Use **quarter notes** (see Book 1 for stem direction rules). Mark the half steps ∧ .

  FJH1170

Writing Major Scales

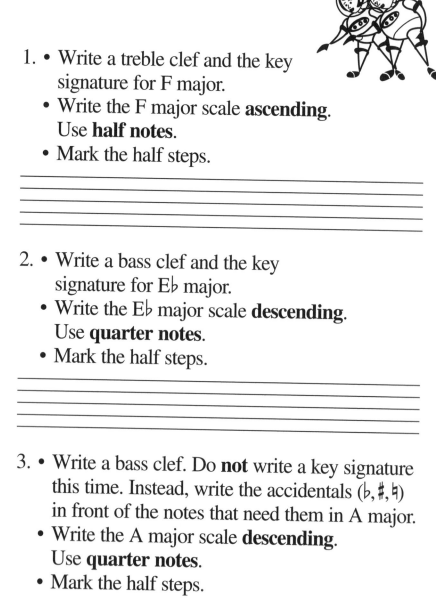

That's major!

1. • Write a treble clef and the key signature for F major.
   • Write the F major scale **ascending**. Use **half notes**.
   • Mark the half steps.

2. • Write a bass clef and the key signature for E♭ major.
   • Write the E♭ major scale **descending**. Use **quarter notes**.
   • Mark the half steps.

3. • Write a bass clef. Do **not** write a key signature this time. Instead, write the accidentals (♭, ♯, ♮) in front of the notes that need them in A major.
   • Write the A major scale **descending**. Use **quarter notes**.
   • Mark the half steps.

4. • Write a treble clef and the key
     signature for G major.
   • Write the G major scale **ascending**.
     Use **whole notes**.
   • Mark the half steps.

5. • Write a bass clef. Do **not** write a key signature
     this time. Instead, write the accidentals.
   • Write the D major scale **descending**.
     Use **quarter notes**.
   • Mark the half steps.

6. • Write a bass clef and the key
     signature for B♭ major.
   • Write the B♭ major scale **ascending**.
     Use **half notes**.
   • Mark the half steps.

FJH1170

Minor Key Signatures

In this book you will learn 3 minor key signatures: **A minor**, **E minor**, and **D minor**.

1. **A minor**

There are *no sharps or flats* in the key of A minor. A minor is the **relative minor of C major**. (This means they share the same key signature.) If you count up 3 half steps from A, you will reach C.

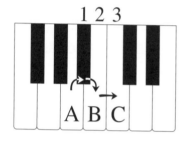

A minor

2. **E minor**

There is *one sharp* (F♯) in the key signature of E minor. E minor is the **relative minor of G major**. If you count up 3 half steps from E, you will reach G.

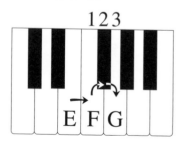

E minor

3. D minor

There is *one flat* (B♭) in the key signature of D minor. D minor is the **relative minor of F major**. If you count up 3 half steps from D, you will reach F.

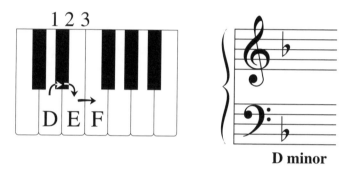

D minor

Practice writing the minor key signatures in both the treble and bass clefs. Don't forget to draw the clef signs.

D minor

E minor

FJH1170

Test Yourself

Fill in the blanks.

1. How many sharps are in the key of G major?

   _____

2. How many flats are in the key of E♭ major?

   _____

3. How many sharps are in the key of A major?

   _____

4. How many flats are in the key of B♭ major?

   _____

5. Which major key signature has one flat?

   _____

6. Which minor key signature has one sharp?

   _____

7. What is the relative major of A minor?

   _____

8. What is the relative minor of F major?

   _____

Write the key signature of:

9. **A major**

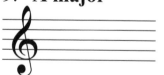

10. **B♭ major**

How many did you get right?

Minor Scales

There are 3 kinds of minor scales: **natural**, **harmonic**, and **melodic**. The easiest minor scale to understand is the **natural minor** scale.

Let's use the example of the E natural minor scale. Notice the key signature of E minor (one sharp, F♯) is already written. Then, starting on the keynote of E, the notes of the E minor scale are written with each note a 2nd apart.

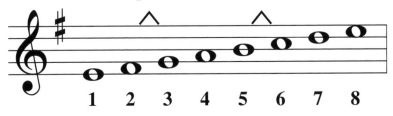

1   2   3   4   5   6   7   8

> In any natural minor scale, there are half steps between notes 2 and 3, and between notes 5 and 6.

Practice writing natural minor scales below.

A minor

D minor

FJH1170

Harmonic Minor Scales

Harmonic minor scales are easy once you understand natural minor.
All you do is **raise the 7th note** of the natural minor scale a half step.

> In harmonic minor, there are half steps between notes 2 and 3, notes 5 and 6, and notes 7 and 8.

Here is the E harmonic minor scale.

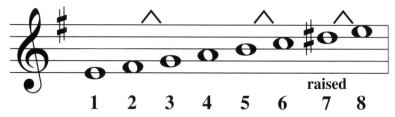

raised

1   2   3   4   5   6   7   8

Practice writing **ascending harmonic minor** scales below. (See p. 19, if needed.)

A harmonic minor

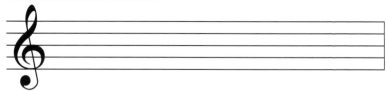

D harmonic minor

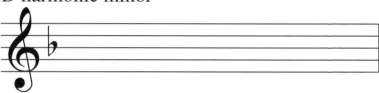

Melodic Minor Scales

Here are easy directions for writing a melodic minor scale.

- First start with a natural minor scale.
- Next, **raise the 6th and 7th notes** in the scale a half step **when ascending**.
- Then, **lower them when descending**.

> In melodic minor, there are half steps between notes 2 and 3, and notes 7 and 8 when ascending. When descending, there are half steps between notes 2 and 3, and notes 5 and 6.

Here is the E melodic minor scale.

Write the **melodic minor** scale below. (Reminder: Remember to use accidentals to lower 6 and 7 when descending.)

D melodic minor

 FJH1170

What's Wrong with these Scales?

Circle the errors in each scale.
(Hint: There will be **two errors** in each.)

1. A natural minor

2. D harmonic minor

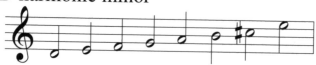

3. D melodic minor

4. E melodic minor

5. E♭ major

Scales on the Keyboard

Write the notes for the following **ascending** scales on the keyboards below. The first scale has been done for you.

1. E♭ major

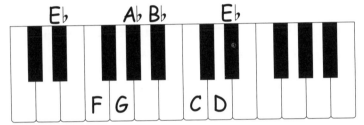

2. A major

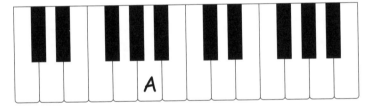

3. E harmonic minor

4. A melodic minor

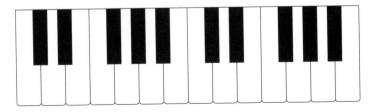

 FJH1170

Key Signature Review

In this book, you have learned the major key signatures and scales up to and including 3 sharps and 3 flats.

You have also learned the minor scales up to and including one sharp and one flat. You will learn more minor keys in Book 3.

MAJOR	KEY SIGNATURE	MINOR
C	no sharps or flats	a
G	F♯	e
D	F♯ C♯	—
A	F♯ C♯ G♯	—
F	B♭	d
B♭	B♭ E♭	—
E♭	B♭ E♭ A♭	—

Scale Degrees

In Book 1, you learned that the first note of a scale is called the **keynote** or the **1st degree**.

The second note of the scale is called the 2nd degree. The third note is the 3rd degree, and so on until you reach the 8th degree (octave).

C major

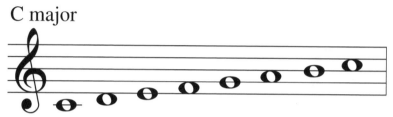

Degrees: <u>1st</u> <u>2nd</u> <u>3rd</u> <u>4th</u> <u>5th</u> <u>6th</u> <u>7th</u> <u>8th</u>

Write the degrees of the scale (1st, 2nd, etc.) under each of the notes in the examples.

D major

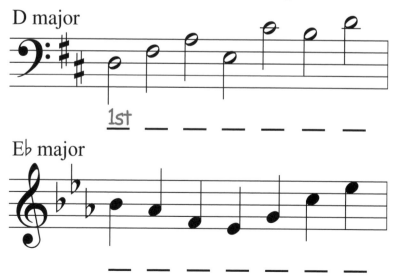

   FJH1170

Intervals

In Book 1, you learned that an interval is the **distance between two notes**.

Another way of thinking about this is that an interval is the number of scale degrees between two notes. In A minor, you count each interval from A like this:

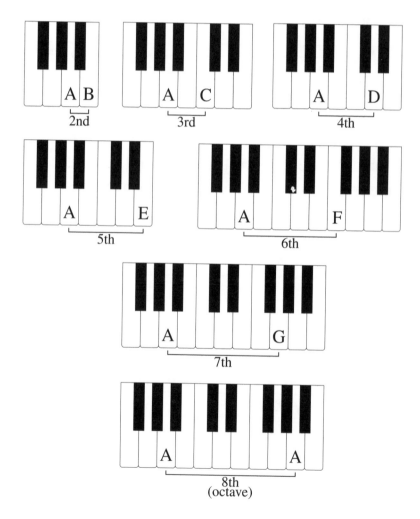

Melodic and Harmonic Interval Review

This is a **melodic interval**:

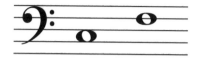

The two notes are written one after the other and are played **separately**.

This is a **harmonic interval**:

The two notes are written one above the other and are played **at the same time**.

FJH1170

Melodic Intervals

In a melodic interval, **always count up from the lower note**, even if the upper note is written first.

Both of the intervals below are a 5th.

Name each melodic interval.

Write the second note to complete each melodic interval below.

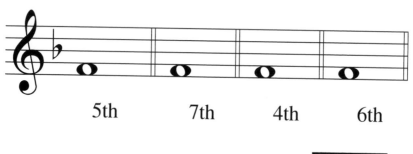

5th   7th   4th   6th

How many did you get right?

Harmonic Intervals

Name each harmonic interval below.

_____   _____   _____   _____   _____

Write the upper note to complete each harmonic
interval below.

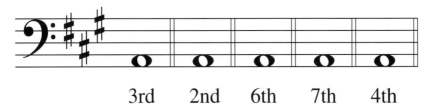

3rd   2nd   6th   7th   4th

How many did you get right?

FJH1170

Tonic Triad Review

In Book 1, you learned that the first note of a scale is called the **tonic**.

A **tonic triad** is made up of three notes:

- the tonic (keynote)
- the 3rd degree
- the 5th degree

Shade in the notehead of the **tonic** for the 4 examples below.

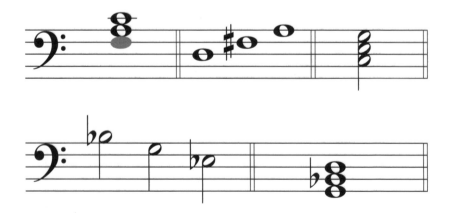

Writing Tonic Triads

Sometimes you may
need to write a tonic triad
with a key signature.

Sometimes you may
need to write a tonic triad
without a key signature.
You'll use accidentals instead.

Practice writing the tonic triads below
with a key signature.

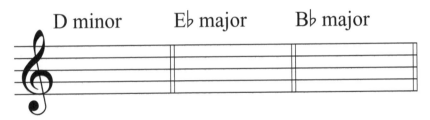

D minor   E♭ major   B♭ major

Practice writing the tonic triads below
without using a key signature.
Remember to add accidentals when needed!

A major   B♭ major   E♭ major

          FJH1170

Test Yourself

- Draw the treble clef, then the key signature.
- Then write the tonic triad.

G major

D minor

F major

A major

E♭ major

E minor

Now write the tonic triads **in bass clef without key signatures**. Remember the clef sign. Add accidentals when needed.

D major

B♭ major

E♭ major

How many did you get right?

Time Signature Review

In Book 1, you learned three time signatures:

$$\mathbf{\frac{2}{4}} \qquad \mathbf{\frac{3}{4}} \qquad \mathbf{\frac{4}{4}}$$

Remember that the top number tells you **how many beats** will be in each measure.

$$\mathbf{\frac{4}{4}}$$

The bottom number tells you **what kind of note** gets one beat. (The **4** means that a ♩ gets one beat.)

Circle each correct answer below.

4/4 *means* **4** or **3** beats in each measure
(circle one)

means the ♩ or ♪ gets one beat

3/4 *means* **4** or **3** beats in each measure

means the ♩ or ♩ gets one beat

2/4 *means* **4** or **2** beats in each measure

means the o or ♩ gets one beat

 FJH1170

More About Time Signatures

Sometimes notes other than quarter notes ♩
will get one beat. For example, in 𝟤/𝟤 time, there
are 2 beats in each measure, and a half note ♩
gets one beat.

Fill in the blanks below.

𝟤
𝟤   means there are _____ beats in each measure.

means a h_____ note gets one beat.

Another name for 𝟤/𝟤 is *cut time*.

It is written like this: 𝄵

Which examples below can be in cut time? Put a
checkmark in the box if it **could** be in cut time.

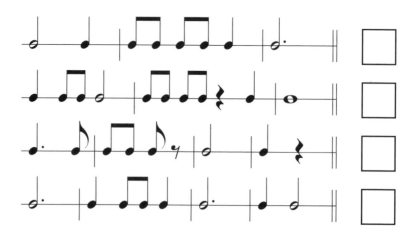

A New Time Signature

Another new time signature is $\frac{3}{8}$.

In $\frac{3}{8}$ time, there are 3 beats in each measure.
The eighth note ♪ gets one beat.

Draw the bar lines to make the examples below correct. Hint: Write the counts first!

```
CHART OF TIME VALUES FOR 2/2 AND 3/8
```

	o or – = 2 beats		♩. or ⁏= 3 beats
2/2	♩ or – = 1 beat	**3/8**	♩ or ⁏ = 2 beats
	♪ or ⁊ = 1/2 beat		♪ or ⁊ = 1 beat
	♪ or ⁊ = 1/4 beat		

FJH1170

Fun with Time Signatures

Draw a line to match each statement with its matching time signature. One has been drawn for you.

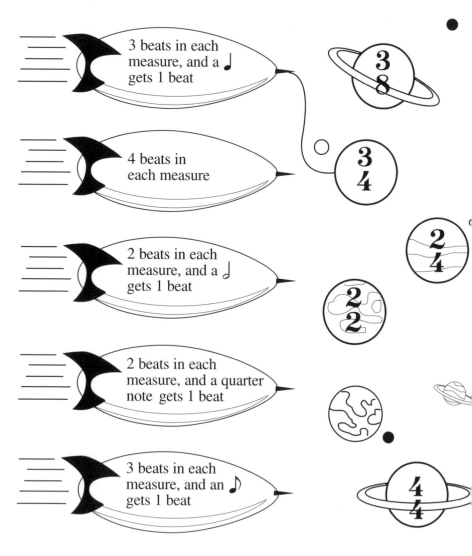

3 beats in each measure, and a ♩ gets 1 beat

4 beats in each measure

2 beats in each measure, and a ♩ gets 1 beat

2 beats in each measure, and a quarter note gets 1 beat

3 beats in each measure, and an ♪ gets 1 beat

3/8

3/4

2/4

2/2

4/4

Writing Rhythm

Write rhythms below. Notice the time signature.
Choose from the notes and rests listed.

> Remember that in any time signature,
> a whole rest ▬ means to rest for the
> whole measure.

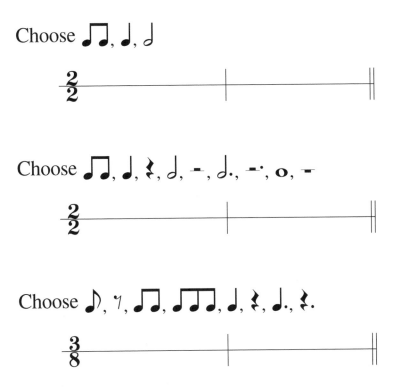

How did you do?

FJH1170

Grouping Notes Review

In Book 1, you learned the rules
for beaming eighth notes.

In $\frac{2}{4}$ time, if there are 4 eighth notes,
they may be beamed together.

In $\frac{3}{4}$ time, you can beam together
a whole measure of eighth notes.

In $\frac{4}{4}$ time, you **can** beam beats 1 and 2,
or beats 3 and 4. You **cannot** beam
beats 2 and 3.

More About Writing
Eighth Notes

To see if you understand the rules from p. 38,
write two measures of eighth notes in the time
signatures given. Make the second measure
different from the first measure in each example.

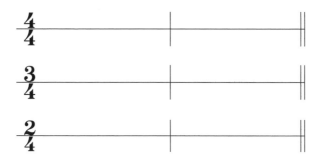

Now you will learn rules for $\frac{2}{2}$ and $\frac{3}{8}$.
In $\frac{2}{2}$, you can beam together 4 eighth notes
following the same rules for $\frac{4}{4}$.

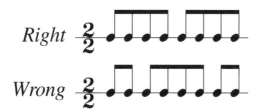

In $\frac{3}{8}$, you can beam together 3 eighth notes.

          FJH1170

More Rules for Stem Directions

When a group of notes is beamed together,
all the stems in the group either go up or down.

You will decide whether to make the stems go up
or down by using the stem direction of the note
that is the **farthest from the middle line**. The
others in the group must follow it.

Turn each set of notes below into a pair of eighth
notes. Remember the stem direction rule!

Time Name Review

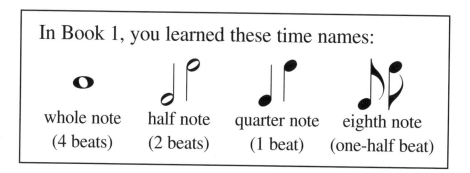

In Book 1, you learned these time names:

whole note (4 beats)   half note (2 beats)   quarter note (1 beat)   eighth note (one-half beat)

The Time Pyramid

The Time Pyramid below shows how the notes relate to each other. For example, you can see that 1 whole note is equal to 2 half notes, 4 quarter notes, and 8 eighth notes.

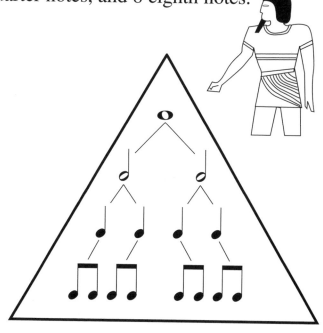

FJH1170

Sixteenth Notes

Sometimes music has notes that move faster than eighth notes.

These notes are called **sixteenth notes**.

Each sixteenth note gets 1/4 (one-quarter) of one beat in $\frac{2}{4}$, $\frac{3}{4}$, or $\frac{4}{4}$ time.

It takes 2 sixteenths to equal 1 eighth.

It takes 4 sixteenths to equal 1 quarter.

Turn each box of quarter notes below into 1 group of 4 sixteenth notes. Hint: You may need to draw more quarter notes.

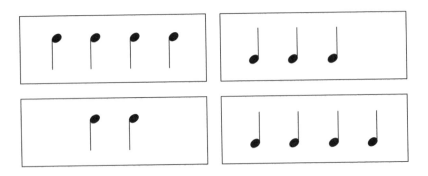

It's About Time

Across

1. Add the beats in $\frac{2}{2}$ time:

   $\textbf{♩} + \textbf{o} + \textbf{♪} + \textbf{𝄽} =$ _____.
   (spell)

4. Four of these equal one quarter note.

6. This rest lasts an entire measure.

Down

1. Add the beats in $\frac{3}{8}$ time:

   $\textbf{♪} + \textbf{♪.} =$ ____.

2. 𝄽 is called a _____ rest.
   (spell)

3. This note gets one-half of a beat in $\frac{3}{4}$ time.

5. Eight sixteenth notes equal how many beats in $\frac{2}{4}$ time?

FJH1170

Sixteenth Rests

In Book 1, you learned about rests. Rests stand for silence, and there is a rest that is equal to every time value note.

	NOTE	REST
Whole	𝅝	▬
Half	𝅗𝅥 or 𝅗𝅥	▬
Quarter	♩ or ♩	𝄽
Eighth	♪ or ♪	𝄾
Sixteenth	𝅘𝅥𝅯 or 𝅘𝅥𝅯	𝄿

On the bottom line of the chart above, you see sixteenth notes and a sixteenth rest.

Trace the sixteenth rests below.

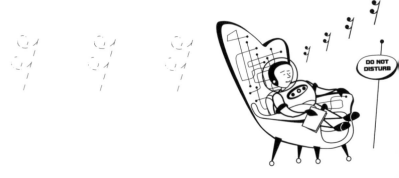

Triplets

A **triplet** is a group of notes or a combination of notes and rests. They equal the time value of two notes or rests of the same kind.

For instance, three triplet eighth notes equal two usual eighth notes.

Or, three triplet quarter notes equal two usual quarter notes.

Triplets may also include rests. Here are examples:

FJH1170

Thinking Triplets

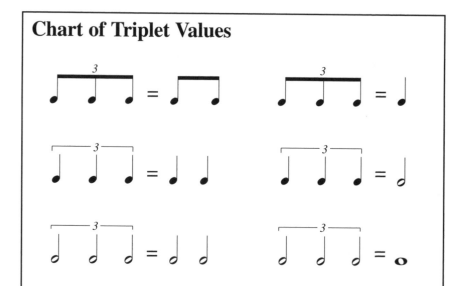

Chart of Triplet Values

Note: You may replace any note above with an equal rest.

For each group of triplets, write **one note** that equals it. Notice the stem direction.

Ledger Note Names

In Book 1, you learned the letter name of the note written one ledger line below the treble clef staff.

You also learned the letter name of the note written one ledger line above the bass clef staff.

Both of these notes sound the same and both are played on the same key: **Middle C**.

Now you will learn notes one more ledger line above and below the treble and bass clef staves.

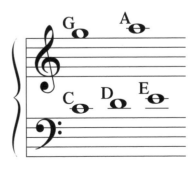

FJH1170

Naming Ledger Notes

Write the letter names for the notes above
each note. Notice the clef sign.

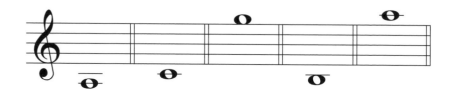

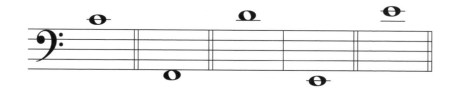

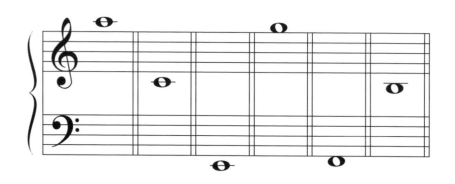

How many did you get correct?

Notes at the Same Pitch

When two notes sound the same, we say they "sound at the same pitch." If playing these notes on the keyboard, we would play the same key for both notes.

Sometimes two notes sound the same, but look different.

For instance, these two E's are at the same pitch.

Write a **bass clef note** that sounds at the same pitch as each treble clef note shown. (Hint: You may wish to imagine a keyboard.)

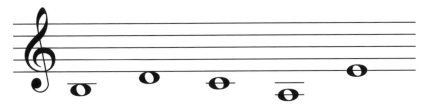

You write:

FJH1170

Abe the Waiter

Once there was a waiter named

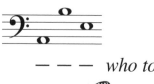

— — — who took the   — — —

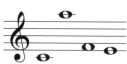

to work each day to the   — — — —.

One sunny day,   — — — saw a sad little

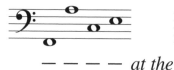

— — — — at the   — — — — window.

— — —, a cute little spotted dog,

was lost and hungry.

FJH1170

He _ _ _ _ _ _ and _ _ _ let him in.

Abe _ _ _ _ _ _ a big juicy steak!

It was lucky that _ _ _ had a collar and a tag.

_ _ _ called the owners, who came quickly.

_ _ _ often came back just to visit

_ _ _ at the _ _ _ _.

The End

FJH1170

Can You Compose?

An important part of composing music is writing the rhythm. See if you can compose (write down) another measure of rhythm for each example. One has been done for you.

Extra Credit: Try to tap and count each rhythm above.

Rhythm Maestro

Draw a line connecting each rhythm pattern
to the correct number of beats.
Hint: *A quarter note gets one beat.*

FJH1170

Musical Matchword

Draw a line to connect two boxes that make one musical word that you know. Then write the word on the blank line.

HARM	ENTAL	_____
TRIP	ADS	_____
LED	VALS	_____
INTER	EENTH	_____
ACCID	LET	_____
MIN	JOR	_____
SIXT	ONIC	_____
MA	ALES	_____
SC	GER	_____
TRI	OR	_____

Musical Scrambles

Unscramble the letters to spell a musical word. Use the clue to help find the answer. Then write the word in the blank box.

ertrqau
Clue: A note worth four sixteenth notes.

(see page 42)

dregle osent
Clue: These are above and below the staff.

(see page 47)

vertinal
Clue: The distance between two scale degrees.

(see page 26)

charmion
Clue: For this interval, play the notes together.

(see page 27)

comidle
Clue: For this interval, play the notes separately.

(see page 27)

pilrett
Clue: Three notes in the time of two.

(see page 45)

icont dratis
Clue: These use the 1st, 3rd, and 5th notes of a scale.

(see page 30)

FJH1170

Musical Crossword

Use the clues below to help you fill in
the crossword puzzle on the next page.

Hint: The dictionary on pages 60 – 62 may help you.

ACROSS

2. Three notes played in the time of two notes.
6. Musical term meaning *not* (see dictionary p. 61).
7. Dots above or below notes are called
    _____ marks.
9. Abbreviation for *ritardando* is _____ (see
    dictionary p. 62).
10. Extra lines above or below the staff.
12. These two notes are sharped in D major.
14. The distance between two notes.

DOWN

1. Raise the 7th note a half step in harmonic
    _____ scales.
3. Symbol means *very soft* (see dictionary p. 62).
4. Built from the 1st, 3rd, and 5th notes of a scale.
5. Raise the 6th and 7th notes one half step when
    ascending in this minor scale.
8. Means *lively, fast* (see dictionary p. 60).
11. Add this to a half note to make it equal three
    quarter notes in $\frac{4}{4}$ time.
13. Symbol means to play smoothly
    (see dictionary p. 62).

FJH1170

Musical Terms Wordsearch

Circle the musical terms below. The Music Dictionary on pages 60 – 62 will help you.

CLUES

1. majestic
2. gracefully
3. sustained
4. very slow and serious
5. too much
6. without
7. less
8. merry, happy
9. loud
10. very

S	A	M	E	N	O	A	C	T	E
O	S	A	G	A	S	B	R	S	I
S	D	J	I	X	O	Z	E	A	E
T	A	S	O	F	I	N	S	H	O
E	W	L	C	R	Z	S	E	N	M
N	H	O	O	A	A	T	D	Y	A
U	J	D	S	T	R	O	P	P	O
T	L	O	O	O	G	R	A	V	E
O	M	E	F	R	O	T	Z	G	T
H	M	A	E	S	T	O	S	O	U

Musical Terms Sentences

Complete each sentence by writing the definition of each musical term. See pages 60 – 62.

1. The principal's words were _____ as he lectured John.
   (grave)

2. "I like butter on popcorn, _____."
   (ma non troppo)

3. She smiled at him _____.
   (dolce)

4. _____, the storm came.
   (subito)

5. The mountain appeared _____ through the clouds.
   (maestoso)

6. The butterfly flew _____ over the sunny meadow.
   (leggero)

7. The elephant is very _____.
   (pesante)

8. "Work at it every day, and you'll get better _____ _____."
   (poco   a   poco)

Dictionary of
Musical Terms

These terms commonly occur in music.

a - at, to, by, for, in the style of

accelerando - becoming gradually faster

adagio - slow, leisurely

allegretto - slightly slower than allegro

allegro - lively, fast

allegro assai - very quick

andante - walking speed

andantino - a little slower than andante
(sometimes faster)

assai - very

a tempo - resume the normal speed

cantabile - in a singing style

col - with

con - with

con brio - with vigor

con moto - with motion

crescendo (*cresc.*) - becoming gradually louder

da capo (*D.C.*) - repeat from the beginning

dal segno (*D.S.*) - repeat from the sign 𝄋

decrescendo (*decresc.*) - becoming gradually softer

diminuendo (*dim.*) - becoming gradually softer

dolce - sweetly

espressivo *(espress., espr.)* - with expression or feeling

fermata - a lengthening of a note or rest

fine - the end

forte (f) - loud, strong

forte-piano (fp) - loud, then immediately soft

fortissimo (ff) - very loud, very strong

forzando (fz) - forced, accented

giocoso - merry, happy

grave - very slow and serious

grazioso - gracefully

larghetto - faster then largo

largo - slow and stately

legato - smooth

leggero (also leggiero) - light, nimble

lento - slow

ma - but

ma non troppo - but not too much

maestoso - majestic

marcato - marked, accented

meno - less

meno mosso - less movement

mezzo forte (mf) - moderately loud

mezzo piano (mp) - moderately soft

moderato - at a moderate speed

molto - much, very

mosso - movement, motion

moto - motion

non - not, no

non troppo - not too much

pesante - heavy

piano (p) - soft

FJH1170

pianissimo (*pp*) - very soft

più - more

pizzicato (*pizz.*) - plucked (for a string instrument)

poco a poco - little by little

portato - semi-staccato

prestissimo - as fast as possible

presto - very quick

rallentando (*rall.*) - becoming gradually slower

ritardando (*ritard., rit.*) - becoming gradually slower

ritenuto (*rit., riten.*) - hold back, slower

scherzando - playful

scherzo - a playful, humorous piece

senza - without

sforzando (*sf, sfz*) - with a sudden strong accent

simile (*sim.*) - continue in the same way

slur - a curved line meaning to play smoothly

sostenuto - sustained

staccatissimo - very detached

staccato - short, detached

subito - suddenly

tempo - speed

tenuto - "held." Hold for entire value of the note; show emphasis to a note or chord

tranquillo - quiet, calm

triplet - three notes or rests in the time of two notes or rests of the same kind

troppo - too much

vivace - lively, quick

List of Music Signs

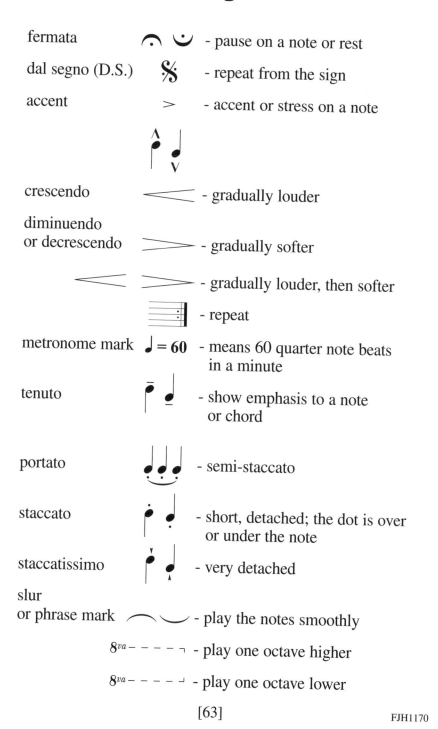

fermata	⌢ ⌣	- pause on a note or rest
dal segno (D.S.)	𝄋	- repeat from the sign
accent	>	- accent or stress on a note
crescendo	<	- gradually louder
diminuendo or decrescendo	>	- gradually softer
	< >	- gradually louder, then softer
		- repeat
metronome mark	♩ = 60	- means 60 quarter note beats in a minute
tenuto		- show emphasis to a note or chord
portato		- semi-staccato
staccato		- short, detached; the dot is over or under the note
staccatissimo		- very detached
slur or phrase mark	⌢ ⌣	- play the notes smoothly
	8ᵛᵃ – – – – ¬	- play one octave higher
	8ᵛᵃ – – – – ⌐	- play one octave lower

[63]

Musical Signs Challenge

Draw the correct musical sign (*ex.* 𝆠 , ⟨).
Use the List of Musical Signs on page 63 to help you.

1. 60 quarter note beats in a minute _____.

2. play one octave lower _____.

3. semi-staccato (portato) _____.

4. play one octave higher _____.

5. pause on a note _____.

6. gradually louder, then softer _____.

7. play the notes smoothly _____.

Progress Chart

Your name: _____
(optional)

✔	Topic	Page
☐	Major key signatures and scales	6
☐	Minor key signatures and scales	16
☐	Scale degrees and intervals	25
☐	Tonic triads	30
☐	Time signatures	34
☐	Grouping notes	38
☐	Time names and rhythmic values	41
☐	Triplets	45
☐	Ledger lines	47
☐	Notes at the same pitch	49
☐	Composing with rhythm	52
☐	Games and puzzles	54

FJH1170

Congratulations to

name

for successfully completing
BLAST OFF WITH MUSIC THEORY!
BOOK 2

on _____
(the date)

Use this staff paper for practice.

FJH1170

FJH1170

FJH1170

THE NEXT STEP?

To get my
Blast Off with Music Theory!
Book 3